Nothing To Do With Skin: The Fundamentals of Epidemiology and Population Health Research

by Raywat Deonandan, PhD

Deonandan Consulting, Inc.
www.deonandan.com
ray@deonandan.com

Copyright © 2014 Raywat Deonandan

ISBN 978-0-9936763-1-4

Deonandan Consulting, Inc, has the exclusive rights to reproduce this work, to prepare derivative works from this work, to publicly distribute this work, to publicly perform this work, and to publicly display this work.

All rights reserved. No part of this publication may be reproduced without the prior written permission of the copyright owner.

Cover image created by George Peter Gatsis (www.georgepetergatsis.com).

What professional Epidemiologists are saying about this book....

"Dr. Deonandan's passion for science and for teaching shows in this book. This book provides a foundation for the exploration of population health sciences and is excellent for teaching new students about epidemiological methods."

-Adam Stevens, MSc
Public Health Epidemiologist
Past President, Association of Public Health Epidemiologists in Ontario

"A readable and very concise basic introduction to epidemiology, with helpful examples. Accessible and often entertaining."

-Nicholas Barrowman, PhD
Biostatistician & Epidemiologist

For my students...
who keep me (more or less) honest.

Table of Contents

Introduction	7
Paradigms of Research	11
Terminology	19
Types of Study Design	23
Hierarchy of Evidence	48
Measurements of Association	51
Correlation and Causation	60
Bias	67
Confounding and Interaction	72
Conclusion	77
About the Author	78

Preface

This book is meant ostensibly as supplementary material for my 4th year undergraduate class in Epidemiology, but is relevant for anyone interested in obtaining a cursory understanding of how we in the population health sciences know what we claim to know. I do not pretend that this is a comprehensive textbook covering all aspects of Epidemiology, but merely an introduction to the basics of our science.

I would like to thank my old friend George Peter Gatsis for contributing the cover image, and would like to dedicate this book to all my students. I came late to academia, as it was never my intended career path. Like most academics, when I decided to become a full-time professor, the last thing I wanted to do was actually teach; it's something we try to minimize in our workloads, preferring to focus most of our energies on research. However, it was an unexpected joy to discover how much I was to learn from the act of teaching, and genuinely how much I cherish my time with students, whose enthusiasm and differing viewpoints never cease to amaze, inspire, and educate me. What a gift it has been to be allowed to become an educator.

I. Introduction

How do we know what we know? That is a fairly profound philosophical question that is beyond the scope of this book. That particular question is the foundation of the fascinating discipline of Epistemology. But in this volume we will explore the basic tenets of that other science that begins with the letter "e": Epidemiology. Yet even Epidemiology, to a very large extent, defines how we as a supposedly science-based society claim to know what we claim to know.

There are too many jokes and stories about the misunderstanding of the word Epidemiology. Almost every practitioner of our discipline has been faced at some point with the honest misunderstanding that Epidemiology has something to do with Dermatology, mostly because of the word "epidermis", which describes a layer of skin. (Or something like that. I don't really know. I'm an Epidemiologist, not a skin doctor.)

The word "Epidemiology" shares the same root as "epidemic". Its origins have to do with the description and analysis of the spread of disease. The official definition is, "the study of the determinants of health", which really doesn't help the layperson understand what we do.

A former professor of mine was held up at a border crossing once, when her profession was noticed by the border official. "Are you transporting any dangerous insects?" she was asked. "No," she had to respond. "I'm an Epidemiologist, not an Entomologist."

Even when the "epidemic" root of our profession is acknowledged, it's not uncommon to have what we do conflated with Virology or Molecular Biology. It's true that some Epidemiologists work in labs and are specialists in infectious diseases. But they are the exception. To be honest, I'm rather disappointed that no one has assumed that my area of specialization is Etymology. I think I would enjoy that conversation.

Another common misunderstanding of our profession is that we are also clinicians. Many Epidemiologists are also physicians, nurses, and other kinds of caregivers. But many more are not. The essence of our science is not dependent upon clinical access or even a deep understanding of Medicine or Biology, although that certainly helps.

Some years ago, a minor Epidemiologist character on the Canadian television show "ReGenesis", which was about bioterrorism, was created. Because of my relationship with one of the writers, to whom I had offered some free scientific consulting, the character was to be named after me: Dr Deonandan. I was initially told that the character would be a very attractive woman. So I immediately began constructing a new psychological diagnosis --that of being sexually attracted to one's own fictional portrayal-- and planned the paper I would write about this new brand of narcissism I had yet to name. Imagine my amusement when Dr. Deonandan's first appearance on-screen showed him to be definitively male and wearing surgical scrubs, just emerging from the operating room. Once again, the Epidemiologist, regardless of gender, had been conflated with the Physician.

There is, without question, a strong clinical side to Epidemiology. Indeed, there is a sub-discipline called Clinical Epidemiology, which is dominated by clinician-scientists. However, this book describes the basic theories underlying population Epidemiology, which is that branch of our science that seeks to explore the manifestation of disease in the general population. In particular, in this book I focus on elements of population health research: study design, biases, and how we measure the association between two factors.

One of the challenges in writing about this subject is not scaring away readers with too much mathematics. Oh, what a sad statement that is! How did we become a society that is afraid of the beauty and poetry of numbers? Regardless, population Epidemiology exists in partnership with Biostatistics, which is that branch of statistical mathematics that allows us to quantify the relationships between factors and influences contributing to health. The use of Biostatistics in this book is minimal. For this reason, this volume should not be considered a comprehensive guide to population research. Rather, it is intended as a companion piece for a more traditional textbook, or an introduction for readers whose interest in the subject is cursory.

The last point I wish to make is that, in my opinion, the principles and techniques of Epidemiology need not be relegated to the world of health research. The essence of our science is logic, and its lessons are applicable to many aspects of life. Similarly, our techniques may be applied to any type of quantitative research, not just those seated within the health domain.

Regardless of what your motivation was for purchasing this book, my hope is that it will help to make you a better informed, more circumspect, and better armed participant in society. If you have any constructive comments to offer, please contact me via my website (deonandan.com) or via Twitter @deonandan.

Raywat Deonandan, PhD
Toronto, Canada
December, 2013

II. Paradigms of Research

In my opinion, the word "Research" is poorly defined and can be used in a variety of quite different contexts. A casual web search can be considered research, as can a cursory discussion with one's friends about an issue of interest. Among scholars, how one views research is profoundly dependent upon the discipline in which one was trained. Anthropologists engage in immersive, subjective types of research that are often not driven by an overt hypothesis or research question. Many social scientists engage in a type of research that is innately qualitative and exploratory, but that does not seek to answer an explicit question; rather, they seek to contextualize observations within a predetermined theoretical framework. As well, particle Physicists seek to elucidate measurable realities about the physical universe through both intellectual cogitation and laboratory experimentation.

In the context of "science", most lay people would view research as lab-oriented, wherein facts about the physical world are derived from experiments whose outcomes are quantified mathematically. A Physicist wears the cloak of science researcher far more comfortably, at least in the public eye, than does a public health researcher. The natural habitat of the scientist is the laboratory, after all. But in reality we are an omnipresent lot who linger and toil in quite varied environments: offices, schools, homes, factories, and farms. To find anything resembling consensus on a definition of the term "Scientist" would require a free afternoon, much argument, and probably a few pints of ale.

The truth is that all of the above styles and environments of inquiry are valid forms of research, and it behooves the humble scholar to give each its due. The scholarship of inquiry can get quite Byzantine if one chooses to explore its philosophical foundations, so I will avoid doing so to any great depth. In its most basic sense, inquiry can be divided into three philosophies: Ontology, Epistemology, and Methodology.[1] Ontology is inquiry into the nature of reality, most fundamentally how we define and experience reality. Epistemology explores the relationship between knowledge and the seeker of that knowledge, specifically the qualities of that relationship that affect or define how the seeker acquires, processes and validates knowledge. And Methodology, the crux of this book, describes the tools and thought structures that determine how knowledge is identified.

A research paradigm is a self-contained set of theories and beliefs that define a philosophical universe of knowledge definition and acquisition. The purposes of a research paradigm can be summarized[2] as follows:

- Define how the world works, how knowledge is extracted from this world, and how one is to think, write, and talk about this knowledge
- Define the types of questions to be asked and the methodologies to be used in answering those questions
- Decide what is published and what is not published
- Structure the world
- Provide the world's meaning and its significance

Given that definition, there are actually several research paradigms that have been described in the academic literature. Three examples are Positivist, Postpositivist, and Naturalist.[1] The differences between these paradigms are debatable, especially since the latter two may be seen as manifestations of the same philosophy. But, in summary, I think it's safe to say that the Positivist approach assumes that inquiry is objective and free of value, whereas Postpositivists accept that the interpretation of reality may be subjectively driven, while Naturalists accept that there may exist multiple realities, each with its own intrinsic value.

Social scientists sometimes pursue Phenomenological inquiry. Investigators in Phenomenology seek to explore a phenomenon or concept without any reference to any existing theoretical framework, deductions, or assumptions. It emphasizes subjects' experiences rather than any deduction from their behaviours or descriptors. It typically uses focus groups or interviews, and is very subjective.

Scholars in the humanities are fond of so-called Post-Modern approaches, which typically involve something called discourse analysis. This analysis stresses the nature of communication. A good way to summarize the intent of discourse analysis is to consider this quote from American poet Muriel Rukeyser: "The universe is made of stories, not of atoms."[3] It suggests that focus on facts alone is insufficient to render a proper sense of things, and that the manner in which we interrogate, consider, process and share those facts are at least as important.

Epidemiology as a science is variably contextualized within a set of competing paradigms. Most common is the Etiologic paradigm, which enjoys a fair amount of overlap with Positivism, and holds that inquiry is intended to identify and quantify causal relationships between factors and a health outcome. One sometimes speaks of the Public Health paradigm, which applies Etiologic principles toward a specific philosophy of purpose that communal good can be achieved through the targeting of population factors that are causally associated with negative public health outcomes.

The point here is that there many ways of looking at research, its intents, assumptions, methods, and interpretations. And while it is impossible to determine which is better or "more correct" without citing the actual methods or philosophies of one of the paradigms being tested, there is nevertheless a political preference for some approaches over others, for reasons that may or may not be defensible.

Beyond the rather arcane discussion of research paradigms, there are a variety of ways to divide up different types of research. One common path is to consider pure versus applied research. The best definition of applied research that I've heard, though its source eludes me, has to do with its practice of exploring a problem, with the explicit intent of contributing to the search for a solution to that problem. So a study that seeks to identify the behavioural causes of testicular cancer is an example of applied research, since its intent is to inform the greater quest to address the problem of testicular cancer.

Pure research (also called basic or fundamental research), on the other hand, has to do with the quest to understand a phenomenon without specific products or applications in mind. Many laboratory sciences and the more philosophical sciences, such as theoretical Physics, would be considered pure research. It is important to realize that pure research very often leads to products and applications years after the initial investigations, though that was never its original intent. For example, our present technological world, so dependent upon microchips, is only made possible by the revelations of Quantum Mechanics, which were discovered from a series of strictly academic laboratory experiments for which a product or application were never considered.

Epidemiology and population health research are, by definition, examples of applied research. Epidemiological studies are formulated for the purpose of identifying or assessing the determinants of disease for the explicit purpose of contributing to the assuagement of that disease.

Another way to categorize research methods is by dividing them into two broad universes: qualitative and quantitative. Mind you, it is also possible to engage methods from both universes simultaneously, in an approach commonly called "mixed methods."

Quantitative research is any methodological approach that involves numbers to which statistical analyses can be applied. Qualitative research, on the other hand, is very difficult to define. A quick web search will render for you many competing definitions. To my mind, the most useful definition is that qualitative research "involves any research that uses data that do not indicate ordinal values."[4] In other words, qualitative research doesn't collect numbers that we can perform math upon.

An example of qualitative research is a series of interviews or focus groups, from which the collected data are opinions or conversations. These are non-ordinal, in the sense that such data cannot be ranked. On the other hand, an example of quantitative research would be the collection of students' ages and IQ scores in a given college class. The resulting numerical data can be prioritized, manipulated, and processed.

The remainder of this book concerns only quantitative research, specifically those types most relevant for population health research. But it behooves a good researcher to be aware of the other types of inquiry that are helping to bring understanding to the world.

References in this chapter:

1. Lincoln YS, Guba EG. (2000). Paradigmatic controversies, contradictions and emerging confluences. In N. K. Denzin & Y. S. Lincoln (Eds.), Handbook of Qualitative Research (2nd ed., pp. 163-188). Thousand Oaks, CA: Sage Publications, Inc.

2. Dills CR, Romiszowski AJ. (1997). The instructional development paradigm: An introduction. In C. R. Dills, and A. J. Romiszowski (Eds)., Instructional development paradigms. Englewood, NJ: Educational Technology Publications, Inc.

3. Rukeyser M. "The Speed of Darkness." From The Collected Poems of Muriel Rukeyser. University of Pittsburgh Press, 2005.

4. Nkwi P, Nyamongo I, Ryan G. (2001). Field research into socio-cultural issues: Methodological guidelines. Yaounde, Cameroon, Africa: International Center for Applied Social Sciences, Research, and Training/UNFPA

III. Terminology

With this book, I endeavoured to avoid using much jargon and technical terminology. Some of it is unavoidable, however. The following is a brief set of important terms and concepts.

A. *Exposure and Outcome*

In classical mathematics, a function typically involves one variable being defined by some computational shenanigans performed upon another variable. For example, the formula for converting degrees Fahrenheit into degrees Celcius is:

$$C = (5/9) \times (F-32)$$

When written thusly, we say that the variable "C" is the dependent variable, while "F" is the independent variable. This is because values of C are defined by the mathematical procedures being done upon values of F, which are free --or independent-- to be whatever they want to be.

In Epidemiology, the analogy of a dependent variable is called an outcome, and the analogy of the independent variable is called an exposure.

Cigarette smoking is an exposure that may or may not lead to the outcome of lung cancer. Whether or not I ate the tuna salad at the company picnic is the exposure that may or may not lead to the outcome of diarrhea. Mathematically, both smoking and the eating of tuna salad are independent variables, while lung cancer and diarrhea are dependent variables.

B. *Incidence and Prevalence*

Incidence and prevalence are two terms that are used interchangeably by the lay person. In population science, however, they mean very different things. Quite simply, an incidence rate refers to the proportion of *new* cases over a specific time period, while prevalence refers to the total present proportion of cases.

We define prevalence as the total number of cases (of a disease, for example) divided by the total number of people in that population. This is usually expressed as a percentage, but can also be given as a rate per total population. For example, in 2013 there were approximately 176 000 cases of prostate cancer in Canada, and a base population of about 35 million. This means that the prevalence of prostate cancer was 176 000 / 35 million or about 0.5%, which can also be expressed as 5 cases per 1000 population.

We define incidence rate as the total number of *new* cases divided by the number of people *at risk for becoming a case*. This means that if you already have the disease, you are not at risk for developing it. The denominator for the incidence rate is therefore smaller than that of the prevalence.

Note that incidence is considered a true "rate" because its denominator includes a measurement of time. Prevalence is a ratio and not a true rate. But some non-sticklers will use the term "prevalence rate", and I don't give them a hard time about it.

Consider a small Sub-Saharan country beset with the disease HIV. The total population of the country is 100 000 people. Each year there are 100 new cases of HIV, and this has been going on for 10 years. Let's say that no one has died or moved away in decades, and no one has been born or immigrated.

At the end of year 10, there are 1000 people living with HIV (100 new cases per year multiplied by 10 years). The total population remains 100000. So the prevalence rate is 1000 / 100 000 or 1% of the country.

That same year, there were 100 new cases. The total number of people at risk for becoming infected was 100 000 minus the 1000 that are already infected, or 99 000. So the incidence rate that year was 100 new cases divided by 99 000 at risk people, or 1/990, or approximately 0.1% per year.

Of course, nothing is this simple. People are moving in and out of the country, and there are births and deaths. And depending on what time of the year we make our calculations, there is a different number of people who have just contracted HIV. We have more precise methods of estimating incidence rates, depending upon these scenarios and upon the size of the overall population.

But you get the picture.

IV. Types of Study Designs

There is disagreement on how best to taxonomize the different styles of study design available to a population researcher. In this chapter, I will describe the taxonomy that I prefer and that I teach to my students. Always remember that how we categorize these designs is ultimately unimportant. Taxonomy serves as an educational tool for helping us to understand the similarities in strengths and weaknesses of various designs. But what matters isn't where a certain design fits along the hierarchy, but whether a given design is most appropriate for a specific research question. In other words, while there are a lot of details in this chapter, don't worry too much if it all starts to get a little blurry in your head.

In general, quantitative research can be divided into three types: Exploratory, Descriptive, and Explanatory. Exploratory research typically concerns an open investigation into a concept or situation that the researcher knows little about. Descriptive studies are applied when the researcher knows a fair amount about the situation, but wishes to describe some aspect in more detail. And Explanatory research, the essence of experimentalism, is an attempt to identify causal factors or pathways.

Epidemiology is a special case of quantitative research. In epidemiological population health research, the unit of analysis is usually a population that can range in size from a handful to millions, and sometimes even to a single individual. In the analysis of the behaviours and descriptors of such groups, the assumption is that nuanced wisdom may be extracted that is relevant to the individual. This is a dangerous statement, and I am wary of perhaps phrasing it imprecisely. There is something called the "ecological fallacy" that teaches us about the perils of attributing to an individual the characteristics that were observed in the group from which that individual was selected. Indeed, in my opinion a major aspect of racism is but a specific type of ecological fallacy, wherein undesirable assumptions about a group of people are assumed to apply to individuals.

So while Epidemiology does not claim to be able to predict outcomes of individuals based upon observations of groups, it does strive to assign probable outcomes to scenarios that have been multiply measured and sometimes manipulated.

In population Epidemiology, the basic type of inquiry is the descriptive study, which seeks --as its name implies-- simply to describe a state of affairs. The following research questions are appropriate for descriptive studies: What is the proportion of women in the national population? What is the average IQ of prepubescent children in Canada? How many human beings have walked on the Moon?

Note that all of these questions have a couple of things in common. First, they are all quantitative in nature, to the extent that they involve the collection of numerical data. Second, no mathematical analyses are being performed between any of the numbers collected. Certainly, proportions, means, medians, etc, of any given one variable can be computed. But the study remains strictly "descriptive" so long as no associations or relationships between two or more collected variables are computed. We are not, for example, determining whether the IQs of pre-pubescent children were correlated with their parents' average incomes.

When relationships between variables are computed, then the type of study is said to be Analytical. Analytical population studies come in two sub-types: Observational and Experimental.

These three types --Descriptive, Observational, and Experimental-- do not map cleanly onto the first three domains that I mentioned: Exploratory, Descriptive, and Explanatory. This is because the Observational types can variably be either Exploratory or Explanatory. Experimental studies are, by the very nature, intended to be Explanatory, however.

The figure below shows the hierarchy of these study types, with the suggestion that complexity, difficulty, and expense run along the x-axis, with experiments being the most complicated and expensive of designs, while descriptive studies are the least complicated and expensive.

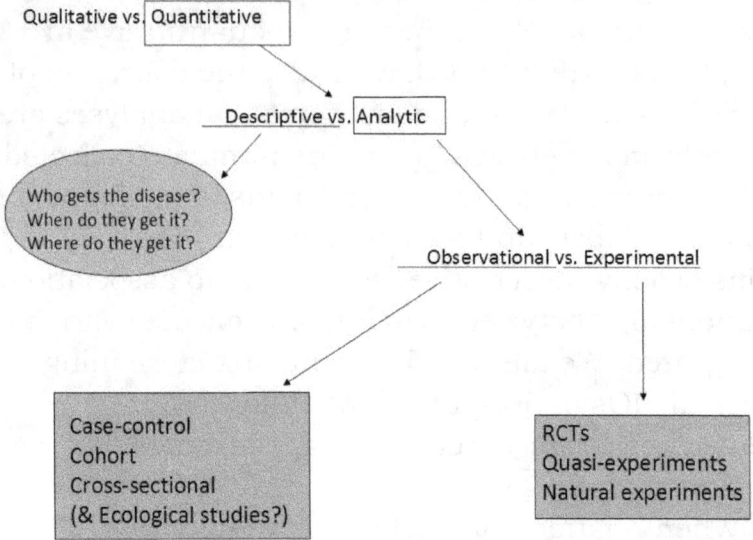

A. *Descriptive studies*

The most common type of Descriptive study in population Epidemiology is the cross-sectional study. And the most obvious example of a cross-sectional study is a telephone survey asking about something that is happening at the moment.

The name "cross-sectional" comes from visualizing the passage of time as a tubular construct moving lengthwise, sort of like a sausage or salami. A single slice of that salami represents a given moment in time. The "cross-section" of that slice tells us all we need to know about the salami at that particular point of its length: its colour, its distribution of ingredients, etc.

Cross-sectional studies, in the form of surveys, are the most common and most basic form of quantitative population research. They qualify as Descriptive in nature if they do not try to associate relationships between two collected variables. For example, a survey question may ask, "Are you politically liberal or conservative?" and "Are you male or female?" If the intent is to determine whether one gender is more likely than the other to be either liberal or conservative, then this cross-sectional study is Analytical, not Descriptive.

Similarly, it is only cross-sectional if facts are ascertained about circumstances at a given moment in time. For example, if I count the number of left-handed students in my undergraduate statistics class, and find that 10% of them are indeed left-handed, then that is a genuine Descriptive, cross-sectional study. But if were to ask each of them if they had ever had a math tutor whilst in elementary school, and tried to associate that fact with their exam marks, then I'm engaging in another type of study entirely.

In brief, Descriptive studies aim to describe a sample of subjects, nothing more.

B. *Observational (Analytical) Studies*

Under my preferred taxonomy, Observational studies are defined as Analytical studies. The defining characteristic of an Observational study is that the researcher does not manipulate the environment in which the research is done. A researcher may select which participants to observe and which aspects of their behaviour to observe, but he or she cannot manipulate the circumstances to elicit responses.

By this definition, it is possible to have a cross-sectional Analytical study. As in the above example, a telephone survey might ask respondents "Are you politically liberal or conservative?" and "Are you male or female?" The post-survey analysis would determine whether one sex is more likely to have a particular political slant. This is clearly an Analytical study since the relationship between two variables is being explored. But it is also clearly an Observational study since the researcher did nothing to make the respondents either liberal, conservative, male, or female. Whether or not the telephone survey had taken place, the respondents' genders and political stances would be the same.

Aside from cross-sectional Analytical studies, there are two broad types of Observational studies. They are called Cohort and Case-Control designs. A good rule of thumb to keep these two separate in your mind is to remember that Cohort studies typically look forward in time, whereas Case-Control studies involve looking backwards in time. However, as will be noted later in this text, many Cohort designs are set in the past in something we call a "retrospective Cohort" design.

i. Cohort Design

The defining characteristic of a Cohort study is that one identifies subjects displaying the exposure of interest, as well as subjects not displaying that exposure, then waits to see which subjects manifest the outcome of interest.

Using our handy smoking/cancer example, in a cohort study one would identify a set of smokers and a set of non-smokers, then follow them forward in time (probably decades) to see which subjects develop lung cancer.

Clearly, with a sufficient sample size, some non-smokers will develop lung cancer. But one will find that the proportion of smokers who develop lung cancer (the incidence rate in the exposed group) will be greater than the proportion of non-smokers who develop lung cancer (the incidence rate in the unexposed group).

The ratio of the incidence in the exposed group to the incidence in the unexposed group is what we call a "relative risk", or RR. The RR is the meat-and-potatoes of a population Epidemiologist, and is one of the most useful and prevalent measures of association. I will explain the RR in a little more detail in a subsequent chapter.

ii. Case-Control Design

A case-control study is the opposite of a cohort study. As the name suggests, a researcher begins by selecting individuals manifesting the outcome of interest (the cases) and individuals not experiencing that outcome (the controls). The next step is to somehow look backwards in time to determine who among the set of subjects had experienced the exposure of interest. This time travel is accomplished through a variety of means, including the examination of medical records and patient interviews.

Let's use our smoking/cancer example again. In a case-control design, we first identify a group of lung cancer patients (cases) and a group without lung cancer (controls). Then we ascertain (probably through patient interviews) what proportion of the cases had smoked earlier in life, and what proportion of the controls had smoked earlier in life. Comparing those two proportions allows us to determine whether those with lung cancer were more likely than those without lung cancer to have smoked.

There are a couple of key points to remember about the case-control scenario. The first is that, since the researcher is actively recruiting cases and controls, the inclusion criteria applied might bias the sample and the results. So typically we try to make the cases and controls as similar as possible. In our example, a realistic situation would see the cases recruited from a cancer ward, and the controls selected from the same institution. That way we can be reasonably assured that the controls are of the same age, gender, socioeconomic status, and (most critically) health status (minus the diagnosis of lung cancer, of course).

The second subtle point to consider is that since individuals are selected based upon their outcome status (i.e., whether or not they have the disease), we cannot truly use a case-control design to compute incidence rates. This is because incidence refers to the natural appearance of an outcome in a given population over a restricted period of time. A case-control design has pre-determined the proportion of cases in the sample, because we deliberately went out and found those cases.

This is important because the computation of a relative risk (RR) depends on the ratio of two incidence rates. Therefore, one cannot meaningfully calculate an RR for a case-control study. Instead, for such studies we compute something called an odds ratio (OR), which is used to estimate an RR. The RR and OR will be explored in more depth in a later chapter.

iii. **How to choose?**

Cohort and case-control studies are similar in cost, complexity and usefulness. But each has its advantages. A key difference is that with the cohort design, the researcher selects the participants based upon their exposure status (smokers versus non-smokers). Whereas, with the case-control design, participants are selected based upon their outcome status (lung cancer versus no lung cancer).

What this is means is that depending upon which is harder to find --exposure or outcome-- we can choose a design of optimum ease. In the exposure is rare, we want to be able to hand-pick them, so we go with the cohort design. If the outcome is rare, we want to be able to hand-pick those, so we go with the case-control design.

For example, what if we want to study whether walking on the Moon is associated with depression later in life? Walking on the Moon is our exposure, and it's pretty darned rare --only twelve men have done it, as of the writing of this book, and only a few of those are still alive. So we would find those men, add some men who did not walk on the Moon (easy to find), and see whether any of our subjects developed depression later in life.

If we had taken the case-control approach, we would instead have found some depressed old people, some happy old people, then asked all of them if they had walked on the Moon. See the problem? It is highly unlikely that anyone in our sample had walked on the Moon. Since the exposure is so rare, the case-control design is biased against finding any effect whatsoever.

(Note that in this example, the Apollo astronauts who walked on the Moon did so decades ago, and are already in their later years. So it is still a cohort study looking "forward" in time from the point of exposure; but since the outcome is already with us today, we call this a "retrospective cohort" design. A retrospective cohort design still moves forward in time, but did so in the past. We usually use medical records to conduct this type of study.)

As another example, consider the question of whether eating cheese results in Creutzfeldt-Jakob Disease. CJD is a very rare disease, and is the human equivalent of Mad Cow disease. (By some estimates, only 0.05% of the population are even carriers of the prion necessary to cause CJD. Only a fraction of those would ever actually manifest the disease.) If we were to use the cohort design, we would first find some cheese-eaters and some people who do not eat cheese, then watch them for decades to see which ones were to develop CJD. None of them probably will do so, since the disease is thankfully so rare, leading us to a biased conclusion.

The proper design would be case-control, wherein we would find some CJD patients from an institution that specializes in that disorder, add some subjects who are demographically similar, but who do not have CJD, then determine (via interviews or chart review) the proportion in each group that had earlier enjoyed a lifetime rife with cheese-eating.

In short, the rarity of the exposure and outcome often determines which Observational study to employ. As well, the point of the study can determine our choice, With a cohort design, we have subjects selected for their exposure status, and we are waiting for a specific outcome to manifest; but there is nothing preventing us from taking note of other outcomes, as well. For example, we can determine from the same sample whether smoking is associated with lung cancer, emphysema, migraines, depression, and a host of many other outcomes that we can add to the list.

Similarly, in case-control studies we have a set of participants selected for their outcome status; but there is nothing preventing us from "looking in back in time" to examine a list of potential exposures. In our smoking example, we can measure the association between getting lung cancer and having smoked, having worked outdoors, having eaten red meat, having taken intravenous drugs, etc.

This is why case-control studies are so popular amongst outbreak investigations. In such scenarios, we already have people with the outcome in hand, and the question is which exposure among many was the likely culprit. An investigator has identified a group of people who got diarrhea from the company picnic, as well as those who also attended the picnic but did not get sick. Looking back, she can determine which exposure --the chicken salad, the vegetarian chili, or that mysterious bowl of green mush-- had the highest odds ratio associated with diarrhea, and thus provide a pretty good estimation of which food was likely the culprit.

iv. **Ecological Studies**

A lesser known Observational design type is the Ecological study. It is considered a poor design from which very few conclusions can be drawn. In essence, the unit of analysis in an Ecological study is a population, rather than an individual.

For example, a researcher seeking to explore the theorized relationship between exposure to farm animals and chronic respiratory diseases like asthma does not have a large enough budget to identify individuals for a case-control or cohort study. Instead, he looks at rural geographical regions and selects several that are known for their high concentrations of dairy farms, and a few others that are known for their high concentrations of wheat farms. (The latter typically do not involve animal husbandry.) He then looks up the asthma rates for these regions and discovers that communities with high rates of animal husbandry have lower rates of asthma than those with low rates of animal husbandry.

Drawing meaningful conclusions from this type of study is difficult. It might be true that all of the people with asthma in the dairy farm communities actually have little contact with animals. Therefore one cannot draw conclusions about individual experiences. To do so would be to invite something called the ecologic fallacy (also called the ecological inference fallacy), which is a kind of bias that assumes that individuals in a group must have characteristics observed in the group as a whole. Ecological studies, in my opinion, are best employed to provide preliminary data for applying for larger grants that will allow a better study.

C. *Experimental Studies*

The last, and most powerful, of designs is the experiment. The layperson uses the word experiment in a less restricted manner than do Epidemiologists. An experiment doesn't have to take place in a laboratory, and it doesn't have to involve lab coats or whirring machines. (Although those are pretty cool.) The defining characteristic of an experiment is that the researcher deliberately manipulates which subjects receive the exposure of interest.

i. **The RCT**

In Epidemiology, the most important experiment is the randomized controlled trial, or RCT. It is also called a "clinical trial" or a "randomized clinical trial". This is the meat-and-potatoes of the drug discovery industry, and constitutes the lion's share of research (as measured by cost) conducted by pharmaceutical companies.

An RCT involves four basic steps: (1) subjects are randomly allocated to two different groups: the treatment group or the control group; (2) the treatment group receives the exposure of interest, while the control group does not; (3) rates of the outcome of interest are measured in both groups; and (4) if the outcome rate in the treatment group is significantly greater than that in the control group, we reliably conclude that the exposure caused the outcome.

As mentioned, the treatment group receives the exposure of interest. We usually refer to this as the intervention. The intervention can be almost anything: a drug, a course, a stern lecture, a roundhouse kick to the head (ethics pending), etc. The control is more complicated. Classically, the control group either receives nothing, or something called a placebo, which I will discuss a bit more below.

At first blush, the RCT resembles the Observational studies. Like a cohort study, it moves forwards in time. And like a case-control study, it has cases (treatment group) and controls (control group). But there are two very important features that distinguish the RCT from its Observational cousins:

1. Subjects are randomly assigned to one group or another
2. The researcher decides which group gets the exposure and actively introduces it, while assuring that the other group is not exposed

Consider what this means. It assures temporality (the exposure definitely comes before the outcome). It also assures that there was no cross-contamination, since most trials are sufficiently controlled and observed to prevent that possibility. More importantly, the act of randomization accomplishes one very important thing: it maximizes the chance that the groups are as comparable as possible.

What does that mean? Let's say we are testing whether a new migraine drug reduces the incidence of migraine headaches. We have two groups of people. The treatment group receives the new drug, while the control group receives a placebo. But we know that women get migraines more often than do men. So if the control group has more men than the treatment group, then it might simply appear that the drug is reducing the migraine rate, when in fact the reduced rate had more to do with the groups' gender distribution!

All right, you say, that's easily solved. We'll only conduct the trial on women. Or just on men. Or we'll make sure that the two groups have equal numbers of men and women. The same approach can be taken for all the variables that we can think of. For example, older people have fewer migraines than young people; so we make sure that there are equal numbers of old and young in both groups. And people who drink coffee may have more or fewer (depending on whose research you read) migraines than those who don't drink coffee; so we control for coffee drinkers, as well.

In short, we do all our due diligence and we make a long list of factors that might bias or confound our results, and we modify our groups' demographics accordingly. But what about the factors we haven't thought of? What about the things that might interact with our fancy new drug, that maybe the pharmacologists haven't identified yet? There are literally hundreds of possible factors --that we don't yet know about-- that can pollute our conclusion that our new drug reduces migraine rates.

So that is why we must randomize. The act of randomly allocating subjects to the treatment or control group theoretically creates an equal distribution of all factors, known and unknown, within each group. Obviously, this will depend upon sample size, how we recruited our initial participants, and how we are going to conduct the actual randomization (there are several methods to choose from). This is one of the things that makes the running of a proper RCT so very complicated and expensive. But the basic point is that random allocation "washes away" a host of biases, both identified and unidentified.

The best RCTs are blinded. And the best of those are double-blinded. A blinded trial (or single-blinded trial) means that the subjects really don't know whether they are in the treatment or control group. Sure, they know they are in a *study*, but they don't know if they are receiving the intervention (eg, the migraine drug) or something else (eg, the placebo). The reason for this is that human beings are psychologically complicated. If the subject knew she was receiving a real migraine drug, she might get fewer migraines just because of the positive nature of that knowledge. Similarly, if she knew she were receiving a fake drug, her symptoms might get worse due to that knowledge alone. This is the fabled *placebo effect*. Wikipedia defines placebo effect as, "The tendency of any medication or treatment, even an inert or ineffective one, to exhibit results simply because the recipient believes that it will work."

A double-blinded trial is one in which neither the subject nor the researcher knows which group is receiving the real drug. Obviously, a record of the true allocation exists, otherwise one would not be able to analyze the resulting data! But the reason for keeping most of the researchers ignorant is that the subjects can often infer which group they are in simply by reading the reactions of the researchers. People are smart like that.

So what is this "placebo" thing I've been going on about? The word literally means, "I will please," in Latin. A placebo is a treatment that resembles the real intervention in every facet possible, except for the characteristic that is being tested. So in the case of our migraine drug example, the placebo would ideally be a pill that looks and feels identical to the drug being tested: same colour, same size, same taste, same regimen. The obvious reason for this is that the subjects (and researchers) must not be allowed to guess which group they are in. The traditional placebo is the cliched "sugar pill".

The problem with placebos is two-fold. First, one cannot generate a placebo for some interventions. For example, if we wish to test whether regular cranial massages will reduce the incidence of migraine headaches, it is impossible for members in the treatment group not to perceive that they are indeed receiving a cranial massage, and impossible for those in the control group not to realize that they are not receiving those wonderful massages. In such cases, blinding is simply not possible.

Second, placebos can be ethically problematic. If we wish to test a new cancer drug on seriously ill cancer patients, then it is not fair to knowingly expose half of our subjects to fake medication. That would be tantamount to a death sentence. The usual alternative is to give the control group the established standard treatment. What this means is that we are no longer testing whether our new drug performs better than nothing (i.e., placebo), but whether our new drug performs better than the current standard treatment. Not only is this more ethical, it is also more useful. We care less about whether a new thing works than we do about whether it works *better than the thing we already have.*

The science of designing, conducting, and analyzing data from RCTs is rich and deep, and we have barely scratched the surface here.

ii. **Related designs**

There are a few designs that have many of the attributes of experiments, but don't fully qualify. Two of those designs are the Natural Experiment and the Quasi Experiment. Many scholars will conflate these two designs. The latter as a term has only been with us since the early 1960s, after all. But I believe they are sufficiently distinct to warrant separate treatment.

a) Quasi Experiment

In a Quasi Experiment, the researcher is indeed artificially introducing an intervention (which distinguishes this design from Observational studies, and qualifies it as a true Experiment). But the study population is in no way randomly allocated. Obviously, lack of randomization deprives this design of one of the the RCT's most valuable attributes. But Quasi Experiments are enormously useful and popular because of several practical considerations.

Quasi Experiments are usually conducted on large, static populations, and are very useful in testing the effects of social interventions. For example, consider a study trying to determine if radio broadcasts about safe sex truly result in reduced HIV rates in an African city. A good way to conduct that study would be to introduce the radio broadcast in a given city, but to compare resulting HIV rates with a neighbouring city of similar size, economy, and demographics, but which did not receive the broadcast. Clearly, the individuals have not been randomly allocated to one city or another, nor has anyone been blinded. Therefore the design is a lot like an RCT: there are two study groups and an intervention given to just one group. But given that it lacks random allocation, and many of the controls preventing cross-contamination (eg, someone from the treatment city telling his friend in the control city all about the great radio broadcast he heard), it's not quite as good as a clean Experiment. So we call it a Quasi Experiment.

b) Natural Experiment

The best way to define a Natural Experiment is to say that it's a design that takes advantage of an intervention that, while external to the population's everyday experience, was not introduced by the researcher. A good example is the atomic bombs being dropped on Hiroshima and Nagasaki at the end of World War II.

The bombs were dropped. But population researchers did not drop the bomb. The bomb was definitely not a normal experience for the population. Researchers looked at the health effects on the populations of Hiroshima and Nagasaki, and compared them to the health states in comparably sized cities that were untouched by the radiation. The intervention was the bomb, and the "treatment" group was the population of the destroyed cities, while the control group was the population of the selected cities.

It seems cold to reduce such a human tragedy to a clinical-sounding study design name. But that is the nature of a Natural Experiment. Whether it is ethical to derive scientific merit from a human-caused affair that created great suffering is a debate that exceeds the mandate of this book. But research ethics is always something to keep in mind.

c) What's The Difference Between the Two?

Natural Experiments are often conducted in the wake of disasters or unpredicted dramatic events. Quasi Experiments are often used for the purposes of evaluating the effectiveness of policies or intentional social interventions. But the distinction between the two is subtle. It has to do with intent and agency. In a Quasi Experiment, the researcher did indeed introduce the intervention. In a Natural Experiment, the researcher did not introduce the intervention, but capitalized on its introduction.

Sometimes the difference is too nuanced to even matter. For example, what if the intervention is the introduction of a no-smoking policy in restaurants? And the researcher is a government Epidemiologist? The researcher did not enact the policy, therefore one can argue that he is conducting a Natural Experiment. On the other hand, he is an arm of the government which did enact the policy, so maybe this is a Quasi Experiment. I would argue that this scenario is a Natural Experiment, since the policy was not enacted for the purpose of study. But, again, the taxonomy is irrelevant. What matters is that the researcher conducts the study with minimal bias and maximum rigour. What he ends up calling his design has no bearing on the quality of the science.

D. *Systematic Reviews*

A systematic review is a type of literature review that follows very carefully thought-out protocols and limitations. It is an attempt to identify all of the high quality evidence pertaining to a given research question, and to collate that evidence in an objective fashion. The best systematic reviews will be based primarily on double-blinded RCTs with meaningful results.

Systematic reviews in Epidemiology are relevant because of the high number of RCTs and Observational studies of varying quality that address the same or similar issues. For example, if we want to know if Vitamin C supplementation can actually prevent or treat the common cold, a quick literature search will reveal scores of studies that have explored this question, often with contradictory conclusions.

Researchers would then develop a search protocol with hard limitations. Perhaps only RCTs will be considered, and not limited to just studies published in English. Perhaps only double-blinded RCTs published in the past five years will be included, or those published in high impact factor journals. There are many search criteria to consider. But the goal is to reduce the list of sources to a core set of only the best available evidence.

i. **Meta Analysis**

A Systematic Review often includes a Meta Analysis. Often the two terms are incorrectly used interchangeably. But they mean very different things. A Meta Analysis is an attempt to mathematically combine the results of two or more different studies. There are special statistical techniques for doing so. A Systematic Review can exist with or without a Meta Analysis.

E. *Other designs*

The list I have presented is by no means exhaustive. There are scores of creative combinations of design types and variations on each theme. But this list represents the core of most types of research presently being conducted.

V. Hierarchy of Evidence

The purpose of conducting the studies described in the previous chapter is to answer research questions that often have policy implications. There is an underlying assumption in the conduct of applied population health research that the evidence being generated from our work will inform policy decisions, at either the institutional or governmental levels.

It is important to realize, though, that the quality of evidence is no guarantee of its uptake by policy makers. There is an entirely separate discipline at work here, variably called Knowledge Translation, Knowledge Mobilization, or Knowledge Exchange. The question of how to get the best quality knowledge to those in greatest need of it, in a form that is of greatest use to them, is one of great interest to many researchers, funders, and government officials. And clearly I won't be answering it here!

Rather, with that challenge in mind, I will instead present the classic Pyramid of Evidence, long held by Epidemiologists as the appropriate hierarchy of quality:

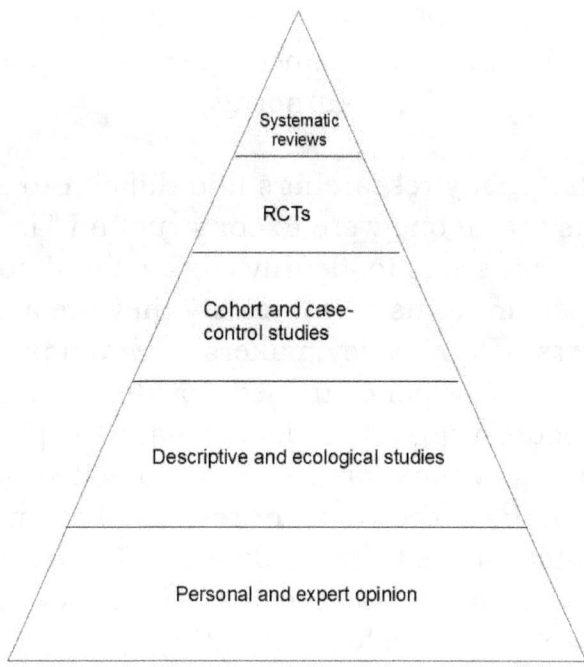

There are many versions of the pyramid. This is my simplified version that I think gets the fundamental points across. The RCT is considered by many to be the "gold standard" of evidence. The only thing of higher quality would be a systematic review of high quality RCTs. Note, as well, that the poorest type of evidence is individual opinion or reliance upon expert opinion and authority.

What many researchers find difficult to accept, though, is that if one were to construct an "accessibility pyramid" that seeks to identify the best and poorest study types, in terms of how easily they are accessed and understood by policy makers, it would probably be the Pyramid of Evidence turned upside down. Despite being of poorest quality evidence, many people, including policy makers, are most motivated by the opinions of those they trust or respect. The importance of exquisitely crafted and analyzed RCTs and systematic reviews might not be fully realized until they are championed by individuals of authority.

These are social and political challenges that are beyond the scope of this book. However, it behooves the researcher to understand the context with which his work will be taken up by those of influence.

VI. Measurements of Association

I promised that this book would be devoid of math. But I wanted to make a quick introduction to two measures that have already been mentioned: the relative risk (RR) and the odds ratio (OR).

Both the RR and OR are measurements of association. This means that they purport to measure how strong of a relationship exists between an exposure and an outcome. Moreover, they purport to measure the extent to which the risk of the outcome is increased in the presence of the exposure. This consideration differentiates the RR and OR from the more common measurement of bivariate relationship, the correlation coefficient.

A. *Correlation Coefficients*

There are many types of correlation coefficients. Most casual users of statistics rely on just two: Pearson's correlation coefficient and Spearman's correlation coefficient. Both are expressed by the Greek letter rho (which looks like a small "r"). Both vary in value from -1 to +1, with the two extremes describing perfect correlation. And both measure the extent to which one variable changes with another.

For example, from birth till the late teens, human height is well correlated with age. That is, the older you get, the taller you get. We say that this is a positive correlation because as one goes up, so does the other. From late middle age until death, the relationship is actually a slight negative correlation: the older you get, the shorter you get. Correlation implies a link of some kind between the two variables. The strength of the correlation is determined by how reliable that link manifests, eg, is the age-height link true at every age?

The difference between Spearman's and Pearson's rho is sometimes difficult for some people to comprehend. But I think it's sufficient to understand that Pearson's rho attempts to describe a linear relationship, while Spearman's rho describes a monotonic relationship.

A linear relationship suggests that every time one variable changes by a certain amount, the other variable will change by certain amount. Consider a car moving along a straight road at a constant speed of 60 kilometres per hour. There is a strong linear correlation between between the length of time the car has been moving and the distance it has travelled. Every hour, the car moves 60 kilometres. The more perfect that linear relationship, the closer that the value of Pearson's rho approaches unity, which is the expression of perfect linearity.

A monotonic relationship, on the other hand, only requires that each variable keep moving in the same direction. The car can be accelerating and decelerating, for example, but it is always moving forward. One hour, the car might go 60 kilometres. The next hour it might go 30. So long as the car doesn't stop and go into reverse, we say that the relationship between time and distance is well correlated monotonically. Spearman's rho describes a monotonic relationship.

Correlations and their close cousins, the linear regressions, are powerful tools for modelling a host of Epidemiological relationships, and are especially useful for making predictions, such as estimating the incidence of certain diseases in a given community.

B. *Relative Risk*

In this book, we are only looking at two associative measurements of risk, though there are several others that are commonly used. Both of these measures --the RR and OR-- are ratios, and therefore can have values ranging from 0 to infinity. If that value is unity (one), then there is no association measured. If that value is greater than one, then we say the exposure is associated with the outcome. And if that value is less that one, we say that that exposure is *protective* of the outcome, meaning that being exposed actually lowers your risk of getting the outcome.

As noted in an earlier chapter, the relative risk (RR) is extremely popular. Also called the risk ratio, it is the ratio of incidence rates in the exposed and unexposed groups.

Let's break it down. If we have 100 smokers, 40 of whom eventually develop lung cancer, we can reliably say the incidence rate of lung cancer in this group is 40/100 or 40%. In other words, the *risk* of getting lung cancer if you are exposed to smoke is 40%.

If we also have 100 non-smokers, only 10 of whom eventually develop lung cancer, then we can conclude that the risk of getting lung cancer when you are *not* exposed to smoke is 10/100 or 10%.

The RR is the ratio of those two numbers: 40/10 or 4. We can interpret this to mean that those who smoke have four times the risk of getting lung cancer than do those who do not smoke. That's a powerful finding. (Keep in mind, of course, that these are fabricated numbers that do not represent any empirical data.)

As with all ratios, the magic number is unity. If RR=1, then there is no difference in the risk rates of the two groups. We use statistics to determine the probability that the RR is significantly different from unity. But my rule of thumb is that anything over 1.5 is an impressive number, while anything from 1.2 to 1.5 is said to have a "weak association". Thus, if RR=4 then that is strong evidence for a relationship between smoking and lung cancer.

C. *Odds Ratio*

As noted earlier, the RR is a ratio of two incidence rates. Incidence can only be calculated forwards in time, since we count the number of new cases as they manifest. Case-control studies look backwards in time and begin by purposefully selecting cases. Therefore incidence rates --and thus RRs-- cannot be computed using case-control studies.

In such instances, we seek to estimate the RR using a construct called the odds ratio (OR). The OR is defined as the odds of the outcome in the exposed group divided by the odds of the outcome in the unexposed group.[1]

To understand the odds ratio, one must first understand odds. The layperson often uses odds and probability interchangeably. But the two are different concepts. Probability is a little like incidence rate (and a lot like prevalence): it's the proportion of selected events out of all the events. So in the example above, the probability of getting lung cancer if you smoke is the number of smokers who got lung cancer divided by the total number of smokers, or 40/100 or 40%.

The odds, on the other hand, is the ratio of events to non-events. If you must know, the formula for calculating the odds from a known probability is:

odds = probability / (1 - probability)

The odds of getting lung cancer if you smoke would be given by the number of smokers who got lung cancer (40) divided by the number of smokers who did not get lung cancer (100-40, or 60). Thus, the odds of a smoker getting lung cancer is 40/60 or about 0.7.

Now, the odds of a non-smoker getting lung cancer is similarly computed. The number of non-smokers who got cancer is 10. The number of non-smokers who did not get cancer is 100-10 or 90. So the odds is given by 10/90 or about 0.1.

The odds ratio (OR) is the ratio of the two: 0.7/0.1 or 7.

How do we interpret this number? Can we say that the probability of getting lung cancer is 7 times greater if you smoke than if you don't smoke? Not at all. But we can say that the *odds* of getting lung cancer are 7 times greater if you smoke than if you don't smoke.

Just like the RR, the magic number is unity. If the OR is close to one, then there is less likelihood of there being an association between the two phenomena.

Why?

Why would we do this? As mentioned, RR does not have any interpretative value for case-control studies. But in our example above, the two computations were so different that one must wonder which measure has more meaning. To answer this question, one must realize that the usefulness of the OR is most frequently as an estimator of the RR. But the caveat is that this is only true *when the disease is rare.*

What is rare? Let's look again at our example above. We have a total of 200 subjects (100 smokers and 100 non-smokers). Among them, there are a total of 50 people with lung cancer (40 among the smokers and 10 among the non-smokers). This gives us a total prevalence rate of 50/200 or 25%. That is a pretty high proportion. Imagine if a disease were to affect a quarter of everybody you know. We certainly would not call that disease rare.

Then let us consider another example in which the disease is much rarer. Let's call this disease Watosis (after your friendly neighbourhood author). And let us attempt to measure an association between Watosis and the drinking of gin (your friendly author's beverage of choice). Let's first consider the data as being from a cohort design: among 100 gin drinkers there are 8 cases of Watosis (incidence rate of 8%); and among the 100 non-drinkers of gin, there were 2 cases of Watosis (incidence rate of 2/100 or 2%). The RR would be 8/2 or 4.

Now let's pretend it's a case-control study and compute the odds ratio. The odds of having Watosis among gin drinkers are given by 8/92 or about 0.09; whereas the odds of having Watosis among the non-drinkers are given by 2/98 or about 0.02. The OR is therefore 0.09/0.02 or 4.5. (If I had used more significant figures instead of rounding up, the actual result would have been closer to 4.26.)

Those two values --4.0 and 4.5-- are not that far apart. This is because Watosis is somewhat rare in this population. Out of 200 subjects, there were only a total of 10 cases, giving a prevalence of 5%. In fact, as the prevalence rate drops, the more the RR and OR converge.

Frankly, 5% is still quite a high prevalence for the types of diseases typically explored with ORs. Many analysts consider a disease to rare enough to use an OR to estimate the RR if the prevalence rate is 10% or less. But, to be honest, that's a pretty high threshold. True rare conditions regularly explored using case-control studies and ORs include ovarian cancer and lupus, which typically have prevalence percentages of less than 1%.[2] When the disease is more common, the OR tends to give a higher value than the RR. Even when the disease is not rare, the OR has a lot of utility beyond simply estimating the RR. But those applications are beyond the scope of this book.

So?

The lesson here is that we have a variety of indexes to measure the relationship between two phenomena. For population risk factors, our favourite tool is the RR. But with rare outcomes and case-control scenarios, we use the OR to estimate the RR. The further these numbers are from unity, the stronger the association between the exposure and outcome.

--

References in this chapter

1. Grimes D, Schultz K. (2008). Making Sense of Odds and Odds Ratios. Obstetrics & Gynecology, 111(2, part 1):423-426
2. Pons-Estel GJ, Alarcón GS, Scofield L, Reinlib L, Cooper GS. Understanding the epidemiology and progression of systemic lupus erythematosus. Semin Arthritis Rheum. 2010;39(4):257.

VII. Correlation and Causation

The mantra oft heard from those with a passing familiarity with statistics is that "correlation is not causation". In class, at this point, usually put on the screen a certain *xkcd* cartoon. (Copyright restrictions prevent me from reproducing it here, but you can follow this link, if you wish: http://xkcd.com/552/).

It's a natural and perfectly reasonable human tendency to draw associations between two phenomena that might not be causally related, just because they tend to occur in similar rates. A classic example is the case of a seaside New England town that maintains reliable statistics on beachfront injuries and confectionery sales. A diligent analyst discovers that when the sales of ice cream went up, so did the incidence of shark attacks! And when the ice sales decreased, reports of shark attacks also decreased.

This is a simple example of what we call "monotonic correlation", which is a specific and straight-forward relationship between two variables. Is it reasonable to then conclude that the selling of ice cream causes sharks to attack people? Or *vice versa*, that after sharks attack, people are somehow compelled to buy more ice cream?

The obvious truth is that both phenomena are responding to another factor: the quality of the day. On nice, sunny days, people are more likely to go to the beach, and are therefore more likely to be bitten by sharks. On those same sunny days, people are also more likely to buy ice cream. One did not cause the other.

The danger of mistaking a correlational relationship for a causal one is obvious. One ends up treating a factor that has no actual effect on the outcome of interest. For example, income is very well correlated with advancing age. This is because most people, as they progress through life, acquire more seniority and experience in their jobs, and are typically rewarded financially. This does not mean that the secret of wealth is old age. A 20 year old going into suspended animation (assuming that such a thing were to exist) and waking up 60 years later would not be automatically wealthy solely due to his advanced age.

A health example is the strong correlation between low income and obesity in the urban USA. Simply giving an overweight person money will not make him slimmer.

Correlation is immensely useful, however. The aforementioned example can illustrate this well. While low income is not the cause of obesity, it is what we call a determinant of health. Policies aimed at improving the average income in an urban community often result in better behaviours among residents, who now have access to expensive gyms and high end grocery stores.

The best tool that a population Epidemiologist has for testing suspected causation is the RCT. If we can control for extraneous factors, as well as the order of events, then we can be reliably assured that a given cause is the likely cause of an observed outcome.

While causation can be inferred in error from a correlational relationship, it's also true that arguments against likely causation are sometimes made for political reasons A good example of this is the now well-known connection between smoking and lung cancer.

Smoking and lung cancer are known to be well correlated. Regions with high rates of lung cancer are also regions with high rates of smoking (an Ecological study). Those who are diagnosed with lung cancer are much more likely to report having smoked in the past than are those not diagnosed with lung cancer. The strength of the observational association between the exposure (smoking) and the outcome (cancer) is great indeed. And yet one cannot logically conclude that smoking is the cause of cancer…. even though we all know that it is.

The reason for this is that it is not ethical to run an RCT on this phenomenon. In our society, thankfully, we are not permitted to randomly assign a group a toddlers to a "non-smoking group", and another group of toddlers to a group compelled to chain smoke for 20 years. In absence of such controlled data, we need a more systematic method for assessing whether a strong association is a likely causal relationship.

There are several packages of criteria that have evolved to give guidance to this process. The most popular is the set of nine criteria, named for Sir Austin Bradford Hill, which describe the minimum set of conditions necessary to describe a causal situation. The criteria are:

i. *Strength*
Is there a measurably strong association (as per our chapter on Measurements of Association) between the putative cause and effect?

ii. *Consistency*
Do you see this strong association when measured multiple times by multiple people in multiple scenarios?

iii. *Specificity*
Can you narrow down the association to a specific group or a specific scenario?

iv. *Temporality*
The cause must precede the effect!

v. *Dose-response relationship*
This is also called a "Biological gradient". It means that the more that the putative cause is present, the more that the effect is observed, and vice versa.

vi. *Plausibility*
Does the observed the relationship make sense, with respect to current scientific knowledge?

vii. *Coherence*

This criterion refers to whether there is any laboratory evidence for the likelihood of a causal relationship.

viii. *Experiment*

Can you refer to any experiments that have been done? Clearly, if an RCT has been done on the topic of interest, there probably isn't any need to appeal to Bradford Hill's criteria. But maybe some experiments have been conducted on animal populations, for example.

ix. *Analogy*

Have you observed similar causal relationships concerning related exposures?

Suitably confused? Let's apply these criteria to an obvious example: the relationship between smoking and lung cancer. Clearly, it is not ethically possible to run a proper RCT on whether smoking causes lung cancer. So society had to rely on Epidemiologists' reading of related criteria to make the causal inference. So let's break it down:

i. *Strength*: The odds ratio of smoking versus not smoking with respect to getting lung cancer is frequently measured as over 100.[1] Anything over 1.5 is considered a strong association. So we can reliably say that the strength is there.

ii. *Consistency:* As per the multitude of studies examining this phenomenon,[1] the association is reliable and consistent.

iii. *Specificity:* While non-smokers do get lung cancer, there is a great deal of evidence to suggest that this malady is largely the specific concern of those exposed to cigarette smoke.

iv. *Temporality:* Certainly, there are almost no instances of people taking up smoking for the first time only after having been diagnosed with lung cancer.

v. *Biological gradient*: The more one smokes, the higher one's risk becomes of developing lung cancer.

vi. *Plausibility*: The theory goes that molecules in smoke damage the cells that line the lungs, making the organ more susceptible to abnormal behaviour.

vii. *Coherence*: Laboratory studies suggest that the chemicals in tobacco smoke have a deleterious effect on cell health.

viii. *Experiment*: Many experiments have exposed cigarette smoke to animals for the purposes of measuring the incidence of cancer.[2]

Conclusion? The putative causal relationship between smoking and lung cancer well satisfies Bradford Hill's criteria. So we can defensibly say that there is strong evidence that smoking causes lung cancer.

It is important to remember that this is but one method of trying to squeeze causality out of a set of observations. Arguments of both deduction and induction have been variably applied. We often limit the application of the Bradford Hill criteria to situations in the health sciences, wherein causality is an important consideration for developing interventions at the population level. In other disciplines, the humanities and social sciences, for example, rendering causality can be less important than a more fruitful exploration of factors associated with a given outcome.

--

References in this chapter:

1. Pesch B, Kendzia B, Gustavsson P, Jöckel KH, Johnen G, Pohlabeln H, Olsson A, Ahrens W, Gross IM, Brüske I, Wichmann HE, Merletti F, Richiardi L, Simonato L, Fortes C, Siemiatycki J, Parent ME, Consonni D, Landi MT, Caporaso N, Zaridze D, Cassidy A, Szeszenia-Dabrowska N, Rudnai P, Lissowska J, Stücker I, Fabianova E, Dumitru RS, Bencko V, Foretova L, Janout V, Rudin CM, Brennan P, Boffetta P, Straif K, Brüning T. Cigarette smoking and lung cancer--relative risk estimates for the major histological types from a pooled analysis of case-control studies.Int J Cancer. 2012 Sep 1;131(5):1210-9

2. Witschi H. Tobacco smoke-induced lung cancer in animals--a challenge to toxicology (?). Int J Toxicol. 2007 Jul-Aug;26(4):339-44.

VIII. Bias

"Bias is a systematic error in the design, conduct or analysis of a study that results in a mistaken estimate of an exposure's effect on the risk of a disease."[1]

In my opinion, the science of Epidemiology is enormously useful to everyone, not only to students and practitioners in the health sciences. A basic understanding of the logic and philosophy of Epidemiology makes one a shrewder consumer, a more insightful individual, and a better citizen. One of the ways this is accomplished is through the digestion of the idea of study bias.

Biases in research can manifest either in the design of a study or in the interpretation of its results. Biases are omnipresent and often serve to either conceal a truth or create the perception of an untruth. There are literally scores of biases that are commonly identified and tackled in population research. But I will only describe five.

A. *Selection Bias*

The most common, and arguably the most important, form of bias is selection bias, or selection effect. The term is used to describe two phenomena:

i. *It's an error due to systematic differences between two groups in a study, ie. between the treatment group and the control group.* If you are conducting an RCT on the effectiveness of a birth control pill, and your treatment group consists of fertile young women, while the control (placebo) group consists of post-menopausal women, your study has been biased, by virtue of participant selection, against finding a positive effect of the drug.

ii. *It's an error due to systematic differences between those who are selected for a study and those who are not.* Imagine you wish to estimate the average height of the American population. So you select 25 Americans and measure their height, take the average, and you're done. But you make the mistake of selecting your sample from an NBA game, and only get professional basketball players whose average height is over 6.5 feet. Clearly, your selection error resulted in a skewed result.

B. *Detection Bias*

Detection bias is one of my personal favourites, as I encounter it frequently in my work in global health. It manifests when a perceived increase (or decrease) in the presence of a phenomenon results from an increase (or decrease) in surveillance of that phenomenon.

For example, after 1996, the incidence rate of HIV climbed quickly in the Caribbean region. This was not as a result of some new behaviour of people or of infected persons migrating to the region. Rather it was due to the initiation of a new HIV surveillance program. In other words, the HIV rate was likely high for some years prior to 1996. But we found new cases because we were *looking* for new cases. In short, finding something might just be the result of looking for that thing. Conversely, not finding a thing might be the result of not looking.

C. *Non-Response Bias*

Ever wonder why people volunteer to participate in medical studies? It's often because they have the time to do so, or they have a vested interest in doing so. The kinds of people who respond to telephone surveys, for example, are retired or unemployed. This is a kind of selection bias, since those participating in the research are demonstrably different from those not participating. This means that any data collected from the participants may not be generalizable to the general population.

D. *Response Bias*

While it sounds similar to non-response bias, response bias is kind of cognitive effect in which respondents in a survey answer questions the way they think the researchers want them to do, or in a way that is more socially acceptable. For example, a researcher is studying the public's knowledge of world geography and asks the question, "Prior to the tragic typhoon in the Philippines, did you know the name of the capital city of that country?" The respondent is socially compelled to answer in the affirmative, even though that might be contrary to the correct answer.

E. *Recall Bias*

People's memories are notoriously unreliable. Recall bias is a systematic error in remembering the past, as it pertains to the collection of data about that past. Consider a real example of a study seeking to measure an association between the MMR vaccine and autism, before and after the media went wild with such speculation. It turns out that the parents of autistic children were more likely to recall that their kids started showing autism symptoms right after being vaccinated in the immediate wake of the publicity, than were parents of autistic kids prior to the publicity.[2] This suggests that the media speculation was encouraging the parents to incorrectly remember the chronology of their childrens' symptomatology.

References in this chapter:

1. Schlesselman J. Case Control Studies: Design, Conduct, Analysis, Volume 2. Oxford University Press,1982
2. Andrews N, Miller E, Taylor B, Lingam R, Simmons A, Stowe J, Waight P. Recall bias, MMR, and autism. Arch Dis Child 2002;87:493-494

IX. Confounding and Interaction

Related to bias are the concepts of Confounding and Interaction (the latter is also known as Effect Modification). The two are oft confused for each other, but are truly distinct effects. A confounding variable is one that either masks or creates the illusion of an association between two other variables, with those latter two variables typically being a cause and effect. An interaction term, on the other hand, is one whose presence simply changes the nature of a real relationship between two other variables.

Technically, neither confounding or interaction are examples of true bias. A rule of thumb is that in confounding, the observation is correct, but the explanation is wrong. And in bias, both the observation and the explanation is wrong. But that's a taxonomical detail. What matters are the concepts, not whether they can be truly considered examples of bias.

A. *Confounding*

Here is my favourite example of confounding: A professor teaches undergraduate statistics to both a Nursing and an Engineering class. At the end of the year, he discovers that 10% of members of his Nursing class are pregnant! He does a quick survey, and discovers that no one in his Engineering class is pregnant. He concludes --erroneously-- that there is a likely causal relationship between studying Nursing and becoming pregnant.

The truth of the matter is obvious to most of us. Despite programs to encourage equal gender representation among various professions, it's still true that the overwhelming majority of Nurses and Nursing students are female. Similarly, a majority of Engineers and Engineering students are male. Therefore, what the professor was really observing was the very real relationship between being female and becoming pregnant.

So we say that the variable of sex has confounded the observed relationship between the topic of the class and the rate of pregnancy. It has created an illusion of a causal relationship between Nursing and becoming pregnant.

How do we test this conclusion? We do so by conducting the analyses separately according to each value of the confounder. So, in the above example, the confounder has two values: male and female. When we only consider the females, the women Nursing students are no more likely to become pregnant than are the women Engineering students; and the male students of both classes are also equally as likely to become pregnant. Therefore we conclude that after "adjusting" for the confounding variable (sex), there is in fact no real difference in pregnancy rates between the two classes.

The following diagram illustrates the basic relationship between a confounder and the other two variables:

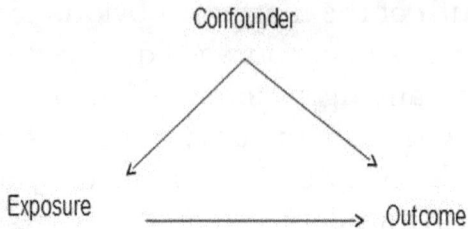

An important aspect of confounding variables is that they do not lie along the causal pathway between the other two variables. For example, consider a perceived relationship between exercise and coronary artery disease (CAD). It is observed that more exercise reduced the risk of CAD. It's also observed that more exercise increases serum levels of high-density lipoprotein (HDL), and that high levels of HDL reduce the risk of CAD.

So is HDL a confounder for the relationship between exercise and CAD? The answer is no, because HDL is actually a mechanism by which exercise reduces CAD. In other words, HDL falls along the causal pathway between exercise and CAD, as per the following image:

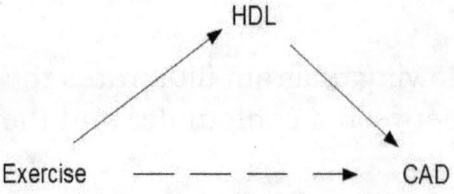

To summarize, then, the characteristics of a confounding variable are: it must have a relationship with the other two variables (i.e., it must definitely be a risk factor for the outcome); it may not lay along the causal pathway between the other two variables; and it either masks or creates and illusion of a relationship between the other two variables.

The classic confounders are:

1. Age
2. Sex
3. Socioeconomic status
4. Smoking status

While this book is not about analytical approaches, I will point out that one of the ways that we control for potential confounding is to break down our analyses by the various levels of the suspected confounder. For example, if we suspect that patients' age is confounding a relationship we are trying to measure between taking a certain drug and eliciting an adverse reaction, we would separate out patients of different age groups: analyze the young separately from the old. In this way, the confounding effect would be removed.

This leads me to the only epidemiology joke I know. Ready? What is an Epidemiologist? Someone who is broken down by age and sex. (Insert rimshot here.)

B. *Interaction*

Many taxonomical sticklers will draw a distinction between interaction and effect modification. Clearly, I tend to use the terms interchangeably. Again, I'm not one for formal details. What matters to me are the fundamental concepts.

Interaction between two variables is said to exist when the association between two variables is different at different levels of a third variable. That third variable is the interaction term, or effect modifier.

Consider the relationship between physical activity and joint mobility. The more active the joint is, the more mobile it becomes. But it turns out that this is only true for young people. Among those above middle age, the more active the joint, the less mobile it becomes. Thus, age is the third variable whose different levels (young versus old) dictates the nature of the relationship between the other two variables: physical activity and joint mobility.

Much like in the case of confounding, a diligent researcher seeks out and tests potential interaction terms and performs the appropriate statistics steps to account for its influence.

X. Conclusion

As I've mentioned a few times, the purpose of this book was to provide an overview of the some of the fundamental concepts concerning population health research, particularly around study design concerns. In future volumes, I hope to go more in depth into exotic designs, methods of randomization, sample size calculation, performing and interpreting statistical analyses, Bayesian techniques, and some of the more esoteric ideas floating about the world of Epidemiology.

This book has been a bit of an experiment, as I decided to forego a traditional publisher and therefore the quality control that such organizations provide. I'm relying upon you, the community of readers to troubleshoot this text. So if you've found an error, or would like to suggest an addition to future volumes, please contact me at my website below or via Twitter @deonandan.

Raywat Deonandan, PhD
www.deonandan.com

About The Author

Raywat Deonandan holds a PhD in Epidemiology & Biostatistics from the University of Western Ontario, and is a faculty member of the Interdisciplinary School of Health Sciences at the University of Ottawa. Since 2009, he has served on the Board of Directors for the Canadian Society of Epidemiology and Biostatistics, and is Editor in Chief of the Society's national newsletter. With a research focus in ethics, global health, and assisted human reproduction, he was formerly the Chief Science Advisor to the agency of the Canadian federal government responsible for issues related to assisted reproduction technologies. Dr. Deonandan makes his home in both Ottawa and Toronto.

www.ingramcontent.com/pod-product-compliance
Lightning Source LLC
LaVergne TN
LVHW051528070426
835507LV00023B/3360